Arowana: The Complete Owner's Guide for the Most Expensive Fish in the World

Arowana Fish Tank, Types, Care, Food, Habitat, Breeding, Mythology – Includes Silver, Platinum, Red, Jardini, Black, Golden, Green

Foreword

The Arowana is the world's most costly aquarium fish. It is a tropical freshwater fish from the brackish swamps of Asia, the river basins of South America, and the pools and billabongs of Austrailia. There are numerous types of Arowanas, most of which can easily grow up to three feet long.

This fish is a savage predator that's been around since the age of the dinosaurs and has remained unchanged, which is why some people call these fish "living fossils." The Arowana is prized for its unique metallic scales; the bristles that bulge from its jaw; and its undulating movements as it swims, which are reminiscent of the paper serpents you might find in a Chinese New Year's parade. In fact, the similarities between the Arowana and the dragon of Chinese lore have given rise to the belief that the fish brings good fortune and success. For all of these reasons, the Arowana has become one of the most coveted aquarium fish in the world.

The situation of the Arowana is very unique: nearly extinct in the wild, Arowanas have actually seen an increase in reproduction in recent years as they're bred by the thousands on farms for the aquarium trade. The Arowana's declining population and subsequent resurgence is a direct result of the conservation movement of the last several decades — but not in the way you might think. In the 1970s, when the international community started to organize around the idea of ensuring imperiled species were protected, the idea was to boycott the exchange of all potentially endangered species, including the Asian Arowana. In those days the Arowana was considered a food fish, and not an especially prized one. Although the interest in Arowanas was relatively minimal at that point, the fish is an apex predator in its ecosystem and a moderate-reproducing species, so it wound up on the list of protected species and was banned from international exchange. This effort at conservation backfired, and spectacularly: once a relatively unpopular food fish, when the Arowana became a restricted species, the interest in it as an aquarium fish spiked. Suddenly, the fish was in high demand as a status symbol, and those in the aquarium trade were eager to breed and raise as many Arowanas as they could for sale.

This brings us to where we are today, with certain prized specimens of Arowana being sold for an astonishing $400,000 each!

What makes this fish so special? We'll discuss the myths, legends, types, costs, and care requirements for the incredibly unique and highly sought-after Arowana.

Chapter 1: What Is An Arowana?

Arowanas are a type of freshwater bony fish of the family Osteoglossidae, otherwise called bonytongues (a group that also encompasses arapaima and knifefishes). Members of the Osteoglossidae family possess a hard, bony head, an elongated body, and large, tough scales. The name "bonytongue" derives from a toothed bone on the bottom of the fish's mouth — the "tongue" — which features small, ridged teeth that can press against similar teeth on the roof of the Arowana's mouth to catch and devour prey.

Arowana species ordinarily develop to around two to three feet in captivity. The Arowana is a facultative air breather, meaning it can acquire oxygen by drawing atmospheric air into its swim bladder, which is lined with capillary tissue much like a human lung.

The Osteoglossidae are the main freshwater fish family found on both sides of the Wallace Line, an imaginary dividing line in the ocean between Asia and Australia that very few freshwater or land species cross. This rare occurrence might be explained by the hypothesis that Asian Arowanas (*Scleropages formosus*) separated from the Australian varieties (*S. jardinii* and *S. leichardti*) around 140 million years ago (Mya), making it likely that Asian Arowanas were conveyed to Asia from Australia via the Indian subcontinent before these continents split apart.

While Arowana classifications are a continuing subject of debate among researchers and aquarium hobbyists alike, there are generally thought to be ten types of Arowana commonly kept as pets: four from Asia, three from South America, two from Australia, and one from Africa (although the African Arowana is not part of the Osteoglossidae family).

The Asian Arowana is common in Vietnam, Cambodia, Thailand, Myanmar, Borneo and Sumatra. It is found in blackwater lakes, swamps, flooded woods, and other waterways with overhanging vegetation. There are several regional variations of the Asian Arowana. The most famous of these is the Super Red variation, which is found only in a few small areas of Western Borneo. The numbers of wild Asian Arowana are consistently diminishing, and as a result, the importation and ownership of Asian Arowanas is restricted in the United States and Australia. Special permission is often required to own these fish in the United Kingdom, China, or Asia.

All members of the Osteoglossidae family are predatory. They are great jumpers; Osteoglossum species have been seen launching themselves more than six feet from the water to pick off insects and small birds from overhanging branches in South America, thus earning them the moniker "water monkeys."

The silver Arowana (*Osteoglossum bicirrhosum*) from South America is the most common type of Arowana. Young silver Arowana fry ordinarily retail cost for $10 or more in most locations, while healthy adults commonly retail for $250 or more. Only the silver and the black Arowana (*O. ferreiral*) can be transported in the United States and Australia. The most sought-after varieties, including the red and golden Arowanas *(Scleropages formosus)* are endangered and cannot be legally imported or owned in most localities. A flourishing black market exists for these fish in some Asian countries; a solitary golden Arowana has a market value of about $1,400 in Indonesia.

The Arowana has a unique reproduction process. In order to reproduce, the Arowana takes part in a two-month courtship and incubation process that results in somewhere between 30 and 80 fry. Many types of Arowanas show an unusual degree of parental care, particularly the males. All species of Arowana are mouthbrooders; the parents sometimes hold hundreds of eggs in their mouths while their young develop. Once hatched, the fry may make several exploratory trips to investigate the surroundings before finally giving up the safety of their parents' mouths for good.

Arowanas are known to be aggressive, and caution must be taken if they will share an aquarium with any other fish. Depending on the temperament of individual fish, many aquarium keepers have had success pairing Arowanas with clown knifefish, pacu, oscars, cichlids (from the same continent as the Arowana; i.e. South American cichlids with South American Arowanas), gars, tinfoil barbs, Siamese tigerfish, and other semi-aggressive fish that can't fit into the Arowana's mouth. Arowanas benefit from a diet featuring a combination of frozen, pellet, and live foods. For most species of Arowana, an aquarium of no less than 250 gallons is a requirement, while tanks upwards of 400-600 gallons are preferable.

Chapter 2: Arowana Myths and Legends

The Asian Arowana (*Scleropages formosus*) is known by many in China and other Asian countries as the "dragonfish." These truly unique aquarium inhabitants are coveted by fishkeepers throughout the world. In numerous legends, the Arowana is considered a symbol of luck, riches and success. Owners of the fish believe that if the Arowana is well cared for, it will protect the owner and their family against hardships and misfortune.

The name "dragonfish" stems from the Asian Arowana's likeness to the mythical beast of Chinese lore. Because the coin-like scales and elegant swimming pattern of the Arowana seem to invoke a dragon, which is itself a symbol of good fortune, the Arowana is viewed as one of the best fish for Feng Shui in the home. It is widely believed that the fish brings a benevolent, nurturing "yang" quality to the residence it inhabits.

It's common for business owners in Asian countries to purchase not only one Arowana, but nine. Purchasing nine Asian Arowanas is believed to ensure that the company will always remain in business. This widespread belief is tied to the fact that the Mandarin word for the number nine ("jiu") also signifies "long-lasting." The number nine is closely tied with a number of myths relating to dragons, including the legend of the Dragon King, who had nine children. The Dragon King himself is considered to have nine forms, and is described in nine attributes.

Another common belief relating to Arowanas is the idea that the fish will sacrifice its life for its owner. A story tells of a man who kept an Arowana in his home, who was in a serious car accident. Despite the severity of the crash, the man escaped with only a few minor cuts. When he returned home, he found that his Arowana had jumped through the covering on its aquarium and died. Stories like these emphasize the belief that the Arowana can absorb negative energy and misfortune on behalf of its owner.

Many owners of Asian Arowana are positive that the fish understands their intentions and can even influence their lives. Another story tells of a man who kept an Asian Arowana for around eight years. The man promised the fish that if he won the lottery, the first thing he would do would be to buy a huge, beautiful tank for the Arowana. He won the lottery and made enough money to buy the new fish tank two times over. Many owners feel a strong connection to their Arowana, and are certain that they fish understand them just like a human.

Chapter 3: Arowana History

The Arowana is an exceptionally old fish. Its form is largely unchanged since the Jurassic era, more than 150 million years ago. The Arowana lived through the rise and fall of the dinosaurs, and survived with few modifications to its ancient appearance. Through millions of years of evolution, the Arowana is now available to us in pet stores looking much the same as it has for millennia.

Modern-day Arowanas can be found in three different continents: Australia, Asia, and South America. Scientists believe that Arowanas arrived in these various habitats before the continental breakup placed oceans in between the land masses that we recognize as separate continents today. Before the continental breakup, the supercontinent Pangea was the only landmass on Earth, allowing the Arowana to spread through interconnected waterways across Pangea's vast surface.

Pangea first began to break apart 175 Mya. Arowanas have undergone such little differentiation since that time that the fish on all three continents are readily identifiable as the same species, despite nearly 100 million years of isolation.

In terms of relatively modern history, the Arowana species *Osteoglossum bicirrhosum,* or silver Arowana, was discovered and named by Geroges Cuvier in 1829. The Greek term "Osteoglossum" signifies "bone-tongued" (from "osteo" meaning bone, and "glossum" meaning tongue), and "bicirrhosum" signifies "two barbels" — so the scientific name aptly describes Arowanas as a bony-tongued fish with two barbels. The fish is known by several common names, including "bony-tongued fish" or simply "bonytongue," "arawana," "aruana," "arrowana," "dragonfish," and "water monkey."

Many individuals have an interest in owning one of these beautiful fish, but don't realize that certain varieties, particularly of Asian Arowanas, are facing extinction in the wild. The population of Arowanas in Asia has declined rapidly over the past half century. Conservation efforts and a worldwide movement to purchase only captive-bred Arowanas (as opposed to wild-caught) are helping restore the Arowana population in the wild.

Chapter 4: Arowana Habitat

The silver Arowana is found throughout the slow-moving and blackwater floodplains of South America. Their native habitat includes the broad region encompassed by the Amazon River Basin, as well as the Rupununi and Oyapock Rivers. The floodplains of South America often feature extremely shallow waterways that are prone to fluctuations, and sometimes these areas will dry up entirely. As a result, Arowanas have evolved the ability to survive out of water much longer than other fish. Because the Arowana is capable of breathing atmospheric air, it can easily survive on land long enough to move to a nearby waterway if it becomes necessary.

Asian Arowanas live in similar ecosystems throughout Southeast Asia, including blackwater swamps, slow-moving rivers and wetlands. Habitat loss is a serious concern for Asian Arowanas; many experts consider the industrial development of previously wild lands the main contributing factor to the Asian Arowana's endangered status, even more so than collection of Arowanas for the aquarium trade. For example, Arowanas were once quite numerous in the Malay Peninsula, but due to extensive development in this region, their numbers have declined steeply over the past several decades.

The native habitat of Australian Arowanas, including *S. leichardti* and *S. jardinii* (sometimes know as a Gulf saratoga), includes the breadth of the Gulf of Carpentaria drainage system, with the western boundary of their range at the Adelaide River. They are also found in New Guinea. These fish inhabit slow-moving sections of streams and clear, still pools. All varieties of Arowanas cannot travel upriver, as they are not strong enough swimmers to go against a powerful current.

Numerous types of Arowanas have, unfortunately, been brought into the waterways of the United States, particularly in California and Nevada. Considered an invasive species in these areas, Arowanas are not naturally found anywhere in the U.S.; instead, many of them found their way into local lakes and rivers when unprepared fishkeepers could not meet the fish's needs and simply turned them loose.

Because of the extremely high price that Arowanas can fetch in the aquarium trade, these fish are a key economic fixture in the areas where they live. Fishermen in Asia and South America often catch these fish in the wild, sometimes defying protective laws in the process, in order to sell them locally or internationally. Sustainable Arowana capture operations and farms that raise Arowanas specifically for the pet trade provide important income for the people who share the Arowanas' habitat.

Chapter 5: Keeping Arowanas as Pets

As you can see, Arowanas are truly unique fish with a complex evolutionary history and an important place in the cultures of many peoples around the world. All of these aspects have helped to make the Arowana one of the most coveted aquarium fish in the entire world.

There are several distinctive types of Arowana that can be found in parts of South America, Asia and even Australia. While these varieties all have unique considerations and needs, there are some similarities across all types of Arowanas. Here, we've collected some of the basic information that applies to keeping any type of Arowanas as a pet.

It is imperative that the aquarium in which any Arowana is kept has a securely-fitted top that is extremely solid. Arowanas are incredible jumpers; they've been known to launch themselves six feet into the air to capture prey in the wild. Imagine a 30-pound, three-foot fish throwing itself against the lid of an aquarium, and it's easy to see why a solid aquarium top is so important. There have been numerous reports of full-grown Arowanas knocking heavy glass lids off of their aquarium and onto the floor and then jumping out after it. Many Arowanas have met their untimely demise in this fashion.

Arowanas are very large fish, and that means they require *massive* tanks — up to 400 gallons in many cases. At the very least, ensure that the Arowana can easily turn around in the tank (they're not very flexible and could injure themselves if the tank isn't wide enough).

Another key requirement for keeping an Arowana healthy is excellent water quality. Like all fish, Arowanas are susceptible to infection and disease when their water is in less than pristine condition. Arowana owners are encouraged to invest in strong filtration that's built to handle the volume of water in an Arowana's tank (which is often up to 400 gallons). Regular weekly water changes (up to 25%) are required to keep dangerous nitrate levels low.

An Arowana's tank ought to be set in a low-activity area of your home to keep the Arowana from getting frightened by sudden noises or movements. Whenever possible, you'll want to change the light levels gradually in the room where the Arowana has its tank (turn off one light, then another, instead of light to dark abruptly), as rapid lighting changes can spook the fish. A frightened or disturbed Arowana can easily harm itself by ramming the top or walls of the aquarium.

Because Arowanas can be so expensive, and some types are strictly regulated, many high-priced Arowanas sold in the aquarium trade are microchipped. When you purchase an Arowana (particularly an Asian Arowana), it will often come with validation papers that state where the fish was raised (be sure that your fish was farm-raised and not wild-caught!) and that it has been microchipped.

While these considerations apply to all types of Arowanas, there are also some noteworthy aspects that are specific to Asian Arowanas. Namely, because Asian Arowanas are considered endangered, there are widespread restrictions on owning this type of fish. Asian Arowanas are listed on the CITES database of threatened species. They are not lawful to keep or import into the U.S. or Australia because of their CITES status. Check the laws in your region before endeavoring to buy an Asian Arowana. (We'll cover this in more detail in the next section.)

Chapter 6: Is It Legal to Keep An Arowana As a Pet? Licensing and Restrictions on Arowanas

Due to the endangered status of certain types of Arowanas, as well as concerns over invasive exotic species, there are restrictions on importing and owning Arowanas in many parts of the world.

If you live in the United States, you will not be able to keep an Asian Arowana of any kind. The U.S. Fish and Wildlife Service states point-blank that "[t]hese fish may not be imported for commercial or personal pet purposes." Only those operating public aquariums or research institutions have been allowed to keep an Asian Arowana.

Silver Arowanas are less restricted in the United States. However, city, county, and local laws may still place restrictions on the ownership of these fish, so it's important to investigate the applicable regulations in your area so that you don't unknowingly break any laws.

In other countries, Arowanas are more accessible. While Asian Arowanas are also illegal in Australia, it is legal, with the correct certification, to purchase and import Asian Arowanas into Canada, Asia, or the United Kingdom. Again, local laws can significantly influence the process required to own an Arowana, so it's a good idea to check with your local Fish and Game Department or Department of Natural Resources (or equivalent governmental office). If you're having trouble figuring out where to begin, try asking an associate at your local fish store — they'll likely be able to point you in the right direction for the regulations in your region.

Remember that even if Arowanas are not restricted for import and purchase, it is still illegal to release these fish into the local water system. Unfortunately, this is a common issue with species like Arowanas that grow very large; once the fish reaches a size that the owner can no longer comfortably care for, some owners simply turn the fish loose in a river or lake. Not only is this a crime in most places, it's also extremely damaging to the environment, as invasive predatory species can wreak havoc on local ecosystems. If you can no longer provide care for your Arowana, or any other exotic species, contact your local fish store or aquarium. In most cases, any of these places will be happy to help you find a home for the fish rather than see it released somewhere it doesn't belong.

Chapter 7: Arowana Types

As we've noted, Arowanas originate from three different continents and many different regions around the world. To help you decide what type of Arowana might be the right choice for your aquarium, take a look at this breakdown of basic statistics for some of the most common types of Arowanas to be kept as pets.

Red Asian Arowana (Super Red Arowana, Red Dragon Arowana, Chili Red Asian Arowana, Golden Red Arowana)

- **Common name:** Super Red Asian Arowana, Asian Arowana, dragonfish, Asian bonytongue
- **Scientific name:** *Scleropages formosus*
- **Full-grown size:** 36 inches/90 cm
- **Place of origin:** Thailand, Malaysia, Myanmar, Indonesia,

Vietnam, and Cambodia

- **Tank requirements and suggested setup:** These fish require plenty of room to swim. Enhance the tank with rocks, bogwood/driftwood and hardy plants. A disturbed Asian Arowana may tear out plants with poor root systems. The minimum suggested tank size is 55 gallons/220 liters for adolescents; however, a completely developed adult fish will require an aquarium that is 250 gallons/1000s liter or bigger.

- **Compatibility:** At least 6 juveniles can be kept together. Adults are generally much less tolerant of their own kind and should either be kept singly or in numbers of 3 or greater. They may be kept with other semi-aggressive or aggressive fish including barbs and certain tetras, but be warned that Arowanas will often try to eat smaller fish.

- **Required water temperature:** 75 – 86° F, 24 – 30° C

- **Required pH:** pH 7.0 – 7.7

- **Feeding:** Juveniles will eat shrimp, bloodworm, krill, and other live or frozen food, but should be trained to accept pellets and food sticks, as this should be the bulk of their diet. Adults can also be fed smaller fish, cockles, mussels, and crickets.

- **Reproduction:** Asian Arowanas are mouthbrooders, and they are typically bred and reared in substantial bodies of water such as lakes. With extensive fishkeeping experience and under the right circumstances, Asian Arowanas may sometimes be bred in an aquarium setting.

- **Extra information:** Red Arowanas can chiefly be found in the waters of Lake Sentarum and the River Kapuas in Indonesia and Malaysia, and they are among the most popular kinds of Asian Arowana. There are 4 classifications of red Arowana: Blood Red, Orange Red, Chili Red, and Golden Red Arowana. The red shading is first obvious in the fins of young Arowanas and gradually spreads throughout their whole body as they develop.

Green Asian Arowana

- **Common name:** Green Asian Arowana, dragonfish, and Asian bonytongue
- **Scientific name:** *Scleropages formosus*
- **Full-grown size:** 36 inches/90 cm.
- **Place of origin:** Thailand, Malaysia, Myanmar, Indonesia, Vietnam, and Cambodia.
- **Tank requirements and suggested setup:** These fish require plenty of room to swim. Embellish the tank with aquarium-quality driftwood and tough plants. A disturbed Asian Arowana may remove plants with poor root frameworks. The minimum suggested tank size is 55 gallons/220 liters for adolescents; however, adults will require an aquarium that is 250 gallons/1000 liters or bigger.
- **Compatibility:** At least 6 juveniles can be kept together.

Adults are generally much less tolerant of their own kind and should either be kept singly or in numbers of 3 or greater. They may be kept with other semi-aggressive or aggressive fish including barbs and certain tetras, but be warned that Arowanas will often try to eat smaller fish.

- **Required water temperature:** 75 – 86° F/24 – 30° C
- **Required pH:** pH 7.0 – 7.7
- **Feeding:** Juveniles will eat shrimp, bloodworm, krill, and other live or frozen food, but should be trained to accept pellets and food sticks, as this should be the bulk of their diet. Adults can also be fed smaller fish, cockles, mussels, and crickets.
- **Reproduction:** Asian Arowanas are mouthbrooders, and they are typically bred and reared in substantial bodies of water such as lakes. With extensive fishkeeping experience and under the right circumstances, Asian Arowanas may sometimes be bred in an aquarium setting.
- **Extra information:** The green Asian Arowana is normally found in Thailand, Malaysia, Myanmar, Indonesia, and Cambodia. Because of the huge scope of their geographic range, there can be significantly more variation in this type than in other Asian Arowana species. Most of these fish are grayish green, and have a head that is bigger and rounder than other Asian types.

Malaysian Golden Asian Arowana

- **Common name:** Malaysian golden Asian Arowana, Asian Arowana, dragonfish, Asian bonytongue
- **Scientific name:** *Scleropages formosus*
- **Full-grown size:** 36 inches/90 cm
- **Place of origin:** Thailand, Malaysia, Myanmar, Indonesia, Vietnam, and Cambodia
- **Tank requirements and suggested setup:** Allow plenty of space for the fish to swim, especially at the top of the aquarium. Add rocks, bogwood/driftwood and durable plants to the tank. An agitated Asian Arowana may remove plants with poor root systems. The minimum suggested tank size is 55 gallons/220 liters for adolescents; a 250 gallon/1000 liter or bigger aquarium will be required for adults.
- **Compatibility:** At least 6 juveniles can be kept together.

Adults are generally much less tolerant of their own kind and should either be kept singly or in numbers of 3 or greater. They may be kept with other semi-aggressive or aggressive fish including barbs and certain tetras, but be warned that Arowanas will often try to eat smaller fish.

- **Required pH:** 75 – 86° F, 24 – 30° C
- **Water science:** pH 7.0 – 7.7
- **Feeding:** Juveniles will eat shrimp, bloodworm, krill, and other live or frozen food, but should be trained to accept pellets and food sticks, as this should be the bulk of their diet. Adults can also be fed smaller fish, cockles, mussels, and crickets.
- **Reproduction:** Asian Arowanas are mouthbrooders, and they are typically bred and reared in substantial bodies of water such as lakes. With extensive fishkeeping experience and under the right circumstances, Asian Arowanas may sometimes be bred in an aquarium setting.
- **Extra information:** The Malaysian golden Arowana originated from the states of Pahang and Perak in West Malaysia. Variations include Gold, Gold-Head, and Full-Gold, Blue-Based. The Malaysian Golden Asian Arowana is also called a Cross-back, due to the metallic gold line on its back.

Banjar Red Arowana

- **Common name:** Banjar Red Arowana, Asian Arowana, dragonfish, Asian bonytongue
- **Scientific name:** *Scleropages formosus*
- **Full-grown size:** 36 inches/90 cm
- **Place of origin:** Thailand, Malaysia, Myanmar, Indonesia, Vietnam, and Cambodia
- **Tank requirements and suggested setup:** Expansive swimming space is essential. Embellish the tank with rocks, driftwood and hardy plants. An agitated Asian Arowana may tear up plants with poorly developed roots. The minimum suggested tank size is 55 gallons/220 liters for adolescents; adult fish will require an aquarium that is 250 gallons/1000 liters or bigger.
- **Compatibility:** At least 6 juveniles can be kept together. Adults are generally much less tolerant of their own kind and should either be kept singly or in numbers of 3 or

31

greater. They may be kept with other semi-aggressive or aggressive fish including barbs and certain tetras, but be warned that Arowanas will often try to eat smaller fish.

- **Required water temperature:** 75 – 86° F, 24 – 30° C
- **Required pH:** pH 7.0 – 7.7
- **Feeding:** Juveniles will eat shrimp, bloodworm, krill, and other live or frozen food, but should be trained to accept pellets and food sticks, as this will be the bulk of their diet once full-grown. Adults can also be fed smaller fish, cockles, mussels, and crickets.
- **Reproduction:** Banjar Arowanas are mouthbrooders, and they are typically bred and reared in substantial bodies of water such as lakes. With extensive fishkeeping experience and under the right circumstances, Asian Arowanas may sometimes be bred in an aquarium setting.
- **Extra information:** The Banjar red Arowana is distinctive due to its rounder head and yellowish green scales. Banjar reds are often known as Grade 2 Red or 1.5 Red.

Red-Tailed Golden Asian Arowana

- **Common name:** Red-tailed Golden Asian Arowana (often abbreviated RTG), Asian Arowana, dragonfish, Asian bonytongue

- **Scientific name:** *Scleropages formosus*

- **Full-grown size:** 36 inches/90 cm

- **Place of origin:** Thailand, Malaysia, Myanmar, Indonesia, Vietnam, and Cambodia

- **Tank requirements and suggested setup:** Allow plenty of swimming space at the top of the tank. Adorn the tank with bogwood/driftwood and tough plants. An unsettled Asian Arowana may uproot delicate plants. The minimum suggested tank size for adolescents is 55 gallons/220 liters; adult fish will require an aquarium that is 250 gallons/1000 liters or bigger.

- **Compatibility:** At least 6 juveniles can be kept together; 10 or more is even better. Adults are generally much less

33

tolerant of their own kind and should either be kept singly or in numbers of 3 or greater. They may be kept with other semi-aggressive or aggressive fish including barbs and certain tetras, but be warned that Arowanas will often try to eat smaller fish.

- **Required water temperature:** 75 – 86° F, 24 – 30° C
- **Required pH:** pH 7.0 – 7.7
- **Feeding:** Juveniles will eat shrimp, bloodworm, krill, and other live or frozen food, but should be trained to accept pellets and food sticks, as this should be the bulk of their diet. Adults can also be fed smaller fish, cockles, mussels, and crickets.
- **Reproduction:** Asian Arowanas are mouthbrooders, and they are typically bred and reared in substantial bodies of water such as lakes. With extensive fishkeeping experience and under the right circumstances, Asian Arowanas may sometimes be bred in an aquarium setting.
- **Extra information:** The Red-tailed Golden Asian Arowana is most often found in Indonesia. They are more moderately priced than Cross-back (Malaysian) Gold Arowanas since they are more common in the wild; their color is considered less desirable as they are not as gold as the Cross-back. RTGs are known to be somewhat more aggressive than Cross-backs, but otherwise these two varieties are very similar.

Black Arowana

- **Common name:** Black Arowana, black dragonfish
- **Scientific name:** *Osteoglossum ferreirai*
- **Full-grown size:** 48 inches/120 cm.
- **Place of origin:** Negro River Basin (Brazil and Colombia) and the upper Essequibo River Basin (Guyana) in South America
- **Tank requirements and suggested setup:** Be sure to provide ample swimming space for the black Arowana. Embellish the tank with aquarium-ready bogwood/driftwood and solid plants (for example, Amazon swords and giant vallisneria). The minimum suggested tank size for adolescents is 40 gallons/160 liters; adult fish will require an aquarium that is 600 gallons/2400 liters or

bigger.

- **Compatibility:** At least 6 juveniles can be kept together. Adults are generally much less tolerant of their own kind and should either be kept singly or in numbers of 3 or greater. They may be kept with other semi-aggressive or aggressive fish including barbs and certain tetras, but be warned that Arowanas will often try to eat smaller fish.

- **Required water temperature:** 75 – 82° F, 24 – 28° C

- **Required pH:** pH 6.0 – 7.5

- **Feeding:** Juveniles will eat shrimp, bloodworm, krill, and other live or frozen food, but should be trained to accept pellets and food sticks, as this should be the bulk of their diet. Adults can also be fed smaller fish, cockles, mussels, and crickets.

- **Reproduction:** Black Arowanas are mouthbrooders. Because of their huge size, they only reproduce in substantial bodies of water, such as lakes. Black Arowanas are not bred in an aquarium setting.

- **Extra information**: It's best to wait to purchase black Arowanas until after their   yolk sac has been totally absorbed. Juveniles should be no less than 4 – 8 inches/10 – 20cm long when they are are purchased; this will ensure that your fish are hardier and less demanding, and you'll have a better chance of the fish surviving to adulthood. The development rate of a black Arowana is around 2 inches

(5cm) a month throughout their first year, so be prepared to upgrade quickly if you start them off in a small tank.

Blue Arowana

- **Common name:** Blue Arowana, blue dragonfish
- **Scientific name:** *Osteoglossum ferreirai*
- **Full-grown size:** 48 inches/120 cm
- **Place of origin:** Negro River Basin (Brazil and Colombia) and the upper Essequibo River Basin (Guyana) in South America
- **Tank requirements and suggested setup:** Allow for plenty of swimming space for a blue Arowana. Add bogwood/driftwood and strong plants to embellish the tank (Amazon swords and giant vallisneria are ideal). Blue Arowanas may uproot plants that aren't well-established. The minimum suggested tank size is 40 gallons/160 liters for adolescents; 600 gallon/2400 liter tanks, or bigger, are recommended for adults.
- **Compatibility:** At least 6 juveniles can be kept together. Adults are generally much less tolerant of their own kind and should either be kept singly or in numbers of 3 or

greater. They may be kept with other semi-aggressive or aggressive fish including barbs and certain tetras, but be warned that Arowanas will often try to eat smaller fish.

- **Required water temperature:** 75 – 82° F, 24 – 28° C
- **Required pH:** pH 6.0 – 7.5
- **Feeding:** Juveniles will eat shrimp, bloodworm, krill, and other live or frozen food, but should be trained to accept pellets and food sticks, as this will be the bulk of their diet once they're full-grown. Adults can also be fed smaller fish, cockles, mussels, and crickets.
- **Reproduction:** Blue Arowanas are mouthbrooders. Because of their substantial size, they typically only reproduce in substantial bodies of water, such as lakes. Blue Arowanas do not typically reproduce in an aquarium setting.
- **Extra information:** Avoid purchasing blue Arowanas until after their yolk sac is totally gone. They should be at least 4 inches long before you bring them home. The development rate of a Blue Arowana is around 2 inches (5cm) a month during their first year, so make sure you'll be able to provide a big enough aquarium for these fish as they grow.

Jardini Arowana

Common name: Australian Arowana, Pearl Arowana, Pearl Dragonfish, Gulf saratoga

Scientific name: *Scleropages jardinii*

Full-grown size: 36 inches/90 cm (although in captivity, full-grown size is often closer to 24 inches)

Place of origin: Northern Australia and New Guinea

Tank requirements and suggested setup: Jardinis, or Australian pearls, will require ample swimming space, particularly near the top of the aquarium, so choose a tank with a large surface area. Minimum suggested tank size for juvenile Jardinis is roughly 50 gallons, but full-grown Jardinis will require a tank of 180 gallons or more. Use a sand or gravel substrate and provide driftwood (the tannins in the wood will help keep the water pH in the ideal range); other tank embellishments should be limited.

Compatibility: Jardini Arowanas are often aggressive toward other Arowanas, particularly once full-grown, but may be kept with certain types of oscars, plecos, and other types of fish that tend to be non-aggressive, stay mainly in the middle or bottom of the tank, and are large enough that they can't be easily swallowed by the Arowana. Compatibility will largely depend on the temperament of your individual fish.

Required temperature: 76 – 85° F, 24 – 29° C

Required pH: 6.0 – 7.0

Feeding: Jardinis can eat a wide variety of foods, including live, frozen, or dried krill, shrimp, bloodworms, mealworms, crickets, and small feeder fish. Always isolate live foods before feeding it to your Arowana to reduce the chance of infection. Arowana or cichlid pellets or sticks should be the bulk of the Jardini Arowana's diet. Juveniles can be fed once or twice per day, and adults once every other day.

Reproduction: Jardinis are mouthbrooders, and they are known to be very difficult to breed in aquariums. Although not impossible, this should only be attempted by experienced aquarists. Breeding Jardinis will require a tank of 600 gallons or more.

Extra information: Jardinis are typically somewhat harder to find in pet shops than Silver Arowanas, although this is changing thanks to an expanding captive-bred Arowana trade. Jardini Arowanas are sometimes confused with barramundi, a name that was once interchangeable with Gulf saratoga (which is still considered an accurate term for Australian Arowanas); however, barramundi is now recognized as a different species (*Lates calcarifer*).

Leichardti Arowana

Common name: Leichardti Pearl Arowana, Leichardti Dragonfish, Dragonfish, Leichardti Arowana

Scientific name: *Scleropages leichardti*

Full-grown size: 36 inches/90 cm (although in captivity, full-grown size is often closer to 24 inches)

Place of origin: Australia

Tank requirements and suggested setup: Leichardti, will require ample swimming space, particularly near the top of the aquarium, so choose a tank with a large surface area. Minimum suggested tank size for juvenile Leichardtis is roughly 50 gallons, but full-grown Leichardtis will require a tank of 180 gallons or more. Use a sand or gravel substrate and provide driftwood (the tannins in the wood will help keep the water pH in the ideal range); other tank embellishments should be limited.

Compatibility: Leichardti Arowanas are often aggressive toward other Arowanas, particularly once full-grown, but may be kept with certain types of oscars, plecos, and other types of fish that tend to be non-aggressive, stay mainly in the middle or bottom of the tank, and are large enough that they can't be easily swallowed by the Arowana. Compatibility will largely depend on the temperament of your individual fish.

Required temperature: 76 – 85° F, 24 – 29° C

Required pH: 6.0 – 7.0

Feeding: Leichardtis can eat a wide variety of foods, including live, frozen, or dried krill, shrimp, bloodworms, mealworms, crickets, and small feeder fish. Always isolate live foods before feeding it to your Arowana to reduce the chance of infection. Arowana or cichlid pellets or sticks should be the bulk of the Leichardti Arowana's diet. Juveniles can be fed once or twice per day, and adults once every other day.

Reproduction: Leichardtis are mouthbrooders, and they are known to be very difficult to breed in aquariums. Although not impossible, this should only be attempted by experienced aquarists. Breeding Leichardtis will require a tank of 600 gallons or more.

Extra information: Leichardtis are typically somewhat harder to find in pet shops than other legal Arowanas, although this is changing thanks to an expanding captive-bred Arowana trade.

Silver Arowana

- **Common name:** Silver Arowana.

- **Scientific name:** *Osteoglossum bicirrhosum*; sometimes designated *Osteoglossum vandelli*

- **Full-grown size:** 35 inches/90 cm

- **Place of origin:** Amazon River Basin of South America

- **Tank requirements and suggested setup:** While juvenile silver Arowanas can start out in a tank as small as 55 gallons, by the time they are full-grown they will require at least a 250 gallon (946 liter) tank. Keep plants and other decorations to the edges of the tank to allow plenty of space to swim near the surface. A dark substrate, such as black gravel, is ideal for silver Arowanas.

- **Compatibility:** Many fishkeepers recommend keeping Arowanas singly, or in numbers of 3 or more; if there's only a pair, the weaker of the two will receive constant aggression from the stronger. With 3 or more, the aggression will be more evenly distributed, reducing stress to smaller or meeker Arowanas. Fish that occupy the bottom of the tank may be suitable tankmates, depending on the temperament of the fish. Tinfoil barbs, mid-sized tetras, and semi-aggressive South American cichlids may share a tank with a silver or platinum Arowana.

- **Required temperature:** 75.2 – 82.4° F, 24 – 28 °C
- **Required pH:** 6.0 - 7.2
- **Feeding:** Silver Arowanas are carnivores and surface feeders. Silver Arowanas can be fed brine shrimp, frozen bloodworm cubes, crickets, cockles, mussels, and even frogs for full-size Arowanas. Feeder fish are best avoided or offered sparingly, as these fish may harbor pathogens or parasites that could harm your Arowana.
- **Reproduction:** Silver Arowanas are mouthbrooders. Most commonly, these fish are bred in substantial bodies of water and they do not typically breed in aquarium settings.
- **Extra information:** Because silver Arowanas are defensive of their young, collectors will regularly kill adult Arowanas to take the fry. This has caused a threat to the silver Arowana's population in the wild. If you purchase a silver Arowana, be sure to find a reputable source that sells captive-bred fish instead of wild-caught.

Platinum Arowana

- **Common name:** Platinum Arowana, Snow Arowana, or White Arowana

- **Scientific name:** *Osteoglossum bicirrhosum*, the silver arowana. Certain rare strains of the Asian species of Arowana, *Scleropages formosus*, may also be classified as platinum.

- **Full-grown size:** 35 inches/90 cm

- **Place of origin:** Amazon River Basin of South America (for the South American variety); Platinum Asian Arowanas may originate from Thailand, Malaysia, Myanmar, Indonesia, Vietnam, and Cambodia.

- **Tank requirements and suggested setup:** Tank requirements are comparable to that of Silver Arowanas. Allow extensive swimming space, especially at the top of the aquarium. Juvenile Platinums may kept in tanks as small as 55 gallons, but you'll quickly need to upgrade to tanks of 250 gallons or more. Because Platinums can grow so large, be sure that your Arowana has plenty of room to comfortably turn around in your tank; otherwise it could be injured. Driftwood and plants can be used to embellish the aquarium.

- **Compatibility:** Platinum Arowanas are generally kept alone. Pairs of Arowanas are inadvisable, and few aquarists will have the space, or budget, to own a school (at least three or four) of Platinums. Platinum Arowanas can be aggressive towards tankmates, and will tend to eat anything small enough to fit in their mouth. Large plecos or catfish may be acceptable tankmates. In light of the fish's extreme rarity and expense, avoid placing a juvenile Arowana in a tank with anything that has the potential to harm it.

- **Required temperature:** 75.2 – 82.4° F, 24 – 28 °C

- **Required pH:** 6.0 – 7.2

- **Feeding:** These fish can be fed shrimp, bloodworms, cockles, mussels, mealworms, and crickets as occasional supplements; the bulk of their food will be pellets and food sticks. Because the Platinum Arowana is so rare and expensive, it's not recommended to use feeder fish, live frogs, or other live foods that have the potential to introduce parasites and disease to the tank. Be sure to remove sharp tails and shells from shrimp and other foods that could potentially harm the Arowana's digestive tract.

- **Reproduction:** Platinum Arowanas are mouthbrooders. Most commonly, these fish are bred in substantial bodies of water and they do not typically breed in aquarium settings.

- **Extra information:** Platinum Arowanas are among the most expensive and coveted aquarium fish on the planet. They are readily identified by a pure white or white-gold coloration. Platinum Arowanas are generally the same species as Silver Arowanas, but their spectacular scales are a result of a rare genetic mutation that makes them extraordinarily valuable in the fish trade. (More rarely, a genetic mutation may cause an Asian Arowana to be classified as Platinum.) A high-quality, full-grown Platinum Arowana has been known to sell for up to $400,000.

Other Types of Arowanas

While these are the main types of Arowanas that we will focus on in this book, some aquarium hobbyists also keep the African Arowana (*Heterotis niloticus*), which is not a true Arowana but a related member of the bonytongue family.

Chapter 8: The Pros and Cons of Owning Each Type of Arowana

There's no doubt that Arowanas are incredible fish — but that doesn't mean caring for them is easy. Even experienced aquarists sometimes struggle with Arowanas for a number of reasons. For one thing, while you may purchase an Arowana as a small fish of only a few inches, they grow extremely quickly — and then keep growing. A 6" Arowana can outgrow a 40 gallon tank in less than 10 months. Sooner rather than later, you'll need a tank with an 8 x 4 foot design to comfortably house a full-grown Arowana.

Additionally, Arowanas are determined jumpers. Even with a heavy aquarium lid, you could run into problems with the fish knocking the lid off of the aquarium or injuring itself against the top, particularly if your fish is easily spooked.

Of course, we've already talked about some of the things that make these fish so desirable despite their particular care requirements — their brilliant coloration, hypnotic swimming patterns, active nature, and impressive size make them exceptional fish for anyone who's lucky enough to own one.

Let's look a little more closely at the pros and cons of owning several common types of Arowanas.

Silver Arowana

Pros: Silver Arowanas with standard coloration are generally quite inexpensive to purchase in the United States, typically running about $30 for a single juvenile. (True platinum Arowanas can cost vastly more, but these are very rare.) If you're an enthusiast of monster fish (fish that regularly grow over two feet long), silver Arowanas could be just right for you; they're one of the largest species available, regularly reaching three feet and sometimes even more.

Cons: Wild-caught silver Arowanas are a major concern for conservation-minded aquarists; on the other hand, farm-bred silver Arowanas often suffer from deformities and weakened immunities after generations of inbreeding. This can be a wonderful fish to own, if you can find a reputable and honest supplier to sell you one.

Platinum Arowana

Pros: The Platinum Arowana is known as one of the most beautiful fish on Earth. Its pure white metallic scales have made it a legend among aquarium hobbyists. The Platinum Arowana is considered to be the crowning jewel in any aquarium collection.

Cons: True Platinum Arowanas only exist due to a very rare genetic mutation. They are extremely difficult to find, and scams where sellers try to pass off lower-grade Silver Arowanas as Platinums are quite common. A legitimate Platinum Arowana will almost never cost less than $50,000, and prices can easily range into the hundreds of thousands of dollars. As a result, platinum arowanas are considered the most expensive aquarium fish in the world.

Black or Blue Arowana

Pros: The black or blue Arowana is extremely similar to the silver Arowana in most regards, with the added benefit that it lacks the problems that often come from inbreeding. These fish are typically much healthier than silvers, as they are always (with some rare exceptions) wild-caught.

Cons: Black or blue Arowanas are very difficult to get in the aquarium trade, and they continue to suffer substantial population losses in the wild due to irresponsible collection. As a result, purchasing one of these fish for a personal aquarium is both very expensive and potentially damaging to the fish's native ecosystem.

Australian Arowana (Includes Jardini Arowana and Leichardti Arowana)

Pros: These fish are known for being especially beautiful and very active, making them an ideal choice for aquarists who enjoy watching their tank. They're often easier to find and cheaper to purchase than Asian Arowanas, but they still provide the key features that fishkeepers love about the Asian species.

Cons: If you're looking to add an Arowana to a community, it's best to look elsewhere. Australian Arowanas are known for being exceptionally aggressive and intolerant of most tankmates. They make a splendid centerpiece fish on their own, but they're likely to make snacks of any smaller fish in the same aquarium.

Asian Arowana (Including Red, Green, Malaysian Golden, and Red-Tailed Golden, Chili Red)

Pros: This is the archetypal Arowana: not quite as large as some of the others, often not as aggressive, and extraordinarily beautiful, the Asian variety of Arowana is the dream fish of many an aquarist. The rich lore and powerful cultural draw of these fish only add to their appeal.

Cons: The Asian Arowana is illegal to own in the United States and Australia, and may be difficult to procure in other countries as well. As a result, the Asian Arowana is much more inaccessible than other types of Arowanas. Particularly outside of Asia, it may be very difficult, and very expensive, to import these fish.

Chapter 9: Arowana Facts

Now that you've got a general sense of the types of Arowanas and what it takes to care for them, it's time to cover some of the key features of this species as a whole that will help you be a well-informed owner of your Arowana.

- **Arowanas are designed for hunting.** There are two barbels at the tip of the lower jaw that the fish uses as feelers to detect and catch prey. An Arowana's vision is extremely sharp, permitting it to see through the surface of the water in order to strike insects off of branches above. Feeding your Arowana live food will help keep its hunting instincts sharp.

- **They live longer than cats or dogs.** It's common for Arowanas to live to 20 years old in a well-maintained aquarium, and even a 30-year lifespan is not unheard of.

- **They can suffer injury if the tank is too small.** The greatest issue that most aquarists have with the Arowana is damage brought on by insufficient room to turn around in the tank. Arowanas are huge, and not very flexible; they can injure themselves if they lack the space to comfortably change direction. As a rule, the width of the tank should be at least the length of the fish.

- **Like all fish, Arowanas are susceptible to infections and disease.** Anything you add to your tank has the possibility of contaminating your fish. Plants, substrate, and even driftwood or rocks can harbor microorganisms or parasites. Feeder fish are notorious as carriers of disease. Be cautious when purchasing feeder fish for your Arowana, and always isolate them for several days before you introduce them to the Arowana tank.

- **Clean water means stress-free fish.** If your water quality isn't in good shape, your Arowana, and any other fish in the tank, will become increasingly susceptible to infection. Because Arowanas are so huge, they require an enormous water volume for their tank, and they also generate a great deal of waste. As a result, a top-quality filtration system is especially important in an Arowana tank.

Chapter 10: Important Requirements for Keeping an Arowana

There are some requirements that are largely the same across all species of Arowana, and these are conditions that must be met to keep your Arowana happy and healthy. Here's a cheat sheet for the key requirements to owning an Arowana:

- **Tank size:** For adolescents, you can get away with a 55 gallon tank — but this won't last long. Most full-grown Arowanas require a tank of 300 gallons or more. A sturdy, secure aquarium lid is an absolute must.

- **Filtration:** Be sure you have a filter system that's graded appropriately for the volume of water in your tank. Even with good filtration, Arowanas produce a lot of waste, so you'll need to do regular weekly water changes to keep nitrates at safe levels. Remember to always treat new water for chlorine and chloramine before you add it to the tank.

- **Feeding intervals:** Juveniles can be fed up to three times per day, and adults once a day or every other day. See Chapter 16 for more information about feeding your Arowana.

- **Substrate type:** Small gravel; dark rock is preferred.

- **Lighting needs:** Moderate/average lighting needs. Ideally, find an aquarium light that has a gradual shut-off feature; a slow shift from bright to dark will mimic daylight and help keep the Arowana at ease. Drastic lighting changes can startle the Arowana and cause it to injure itself.

- **Temperature:** 75 to 86° F (23.9 to 30.0° C). For a tank big enough to house an Arowana, you'll likely need multiple heaters to sustain a steady temperature. (This is also a handy failsafe in case one heater stops working.)
- **pH:** 6.5-7.0
- **Hardness range:** 8 - 12 dGH
- **Preferred water movement:** Weak. In the wild, Arowanas live in blackwater bogs and floodplains; you can mimic this by keeping the water movement from filters or air stones to a minimum.
- **Tank region:** Top. Because Arowanas are surface feeders, they will spend most of their time in the top third of the aquarium. Keep this area clear and open by trimming back plants. Depth is not important to an Arowana tank, but surface area is key.

Arowanas are a unique species in many regards, but a bit of basic fishkeeping know-how will go a long way. If you're new to the aquarium hobby, you'll likely want to start off with something a little easier to manage (and probably a *lot* smaller). The knowledge that you gain from caring for other fish, such as maintaining a water change schedule, choosing and setting up a filter, and paying attention to fish behavior to identify potential problems, will undoubtedly carry over to help you care for your Arowana in the best possible way.

Although we've summarized the basic care requirements of an Arowana here, there's far more to it than these bullet points. (After all, that's why we wrote a whole book about it!) While an Arowana is many aquarists' dream fish, it's important to emphasis it's not an ideal fish for beginners.

Chapter 11: The Benefits of Keeping an Arowana for Physical and Spiritual Health

Aquariums are not just decorations for your home or office. In recent years, scientists have demonstrated that keeping fish in an aquarium provides numerous health benefits to the owner. Spending just a few minutes watching fish in an aquarium has been shown to reduce stress and induce relaxation.

Medical Benefits of Owning an Arowana

Have you ever wondered why fish tanks are so common in dentists' offices? The soothing effect of aquariums is exactly the reason that so many medical offices feature a fish tank in their waiting room: the presence of an aquarium has been proven to ease the anxiety of nervous patients. In fact, research into this phenomenon has shown that patients who watched an aquarium after a procedure required fewer painkillers than those who didn't.

People with hypertension and children diagnosed with ADHD had a particularly positive reaction to aquariums, with noticeably higher levels of calmness and relaxation simply by being in the same room with an aquarium. Unlike the medications that are used to treat these conditions, aquariums have zero unpleasant side effects while still offering the same benefit as a prescription drug.

If you choose to get an Arowana, remember that you can't enjoy the benefits of owning one without putting in the work. To truly take advantage of all that an Arowana can offer, you have to make sure the fish is as happy and healthy as it can be. That way, you'll be drawing out the best in the fish and ensuring that you can enjoy its presence to the fullest extent. With an initial investment of time, money, and energy, you'll be on your way to enjoying the mental, physical, and even spiritual benefits of this incredible fish.

Spiritual Benefits of Owning an Arowana

In Chinese folklore, it is widely believed that winged serpents protect against malicious spirits and ensure good fortune. This belief in the benevolent power of winged serpents is the reason behind the popularity of the Asian Arowana. Also called the dragonfish due to its similarity to the legendary creature, the Asian Arowana is widely believed to convey favorable luck to whoever owns it. Many business owners keep an Asian Arowana, particularly the Malaysian Gold variety, to ensure that their business is successful and prosperous.

Many Chinese Arowana owners believe that the Arowana can serve as a bellwether to ensure the health and protection of the family. A common belief holds that an Arowana can distinguish the people who wish to do harm to the owner or the owner's family. If a visitor enters the home and the fish begins to flail or show distress, that visitor has malicious intentions for the family. On the other hand, if the fish remains quiet and composed when a new visitor arrives, that person is considered to be a friend to the family.

Because of its gorgeous coloration and metallic, coin-like scales, the Arowana is considered to possess the dragon's powers of attracting success, riches, and good fortune. Admirers of Arowanas are often so certain in its ability to bring blessings that some will display a picture of the fish in their home, even if they don't own one, in the belief that simply representing the Arowana can have a positive effect.

The Role of Arowana in Feng Shui

Feng shui is an ancient Chinese belief system rooted in Taoism. It is focused on bringing individuals into harmony with their environment by arranging one's living space in accordance with different types of energies to achieve balance. Feng shui literally translates as "wind-water," so it's no surprise that aquariums hold an important place in this tradition.

Water is believed to store or collect qi, or life force. Because the Arowana is so closely tied to the dragon of Chinese mythology, it is considered to represent success and good fortune. Therefore, the combination of qi represented by the water and the positive associations represented by the Arowana are believed to be a powerful union in creating desirable outcomes for the owner of the aquarium. When deciding where to place the winged serpent fish, according to feng shui principles, it ought to be kept in an eastern, northern, or southeastern area of your office or home. Feng shui practitioners believe that Arowanas should never be placed in the northwest or west areas of a house, as these areas can counteract the positive impact of bringing the Arowana into your home. It is also not advisable to keep an Arowana in a bedroom or kitchen, as this may invite money problems or sickness into the owner's life.

Chapter 12: Negative Aspects of Owning an Arowana

Although there's no doubt that Arowanas are exceptionally beautiful fish, with glimmering metallic scales, a positively Jurassic appearance and hypnotic, serpent-like movements, they are certainly not the right fish for everyone.

The first thing that will likely discourage people from purchasing an Arowana is the cost. Compared to the vast majority of other aquarium fish, including most cichlids, oscars, and other freshwater centerpiece fish, even the smallest and most common Arowanas start out relatively expensive and increase in cost rapidly. The least you would be likely to pay for one of these fish would be $30 for a very small, 2-3" silver Arowana. Prices for larger specimens, and those from a rarer species such as blue, black, or any type of Asian Arowana, will quickly spike into the hundreds or even thousands of dollars. Add on top of that the cost of the tank, the filter, the heater, the aquarium cover, the water conditioners, the substrate, plants, thermometer, and everything else that it takes to keep a tank up and running — it's easy to see why owning an Arowana is often an investment of many thousands of dollars.

Additionally, these fish require an enormous amount of space; a

500 gallon tank, which is recommended for many types of full-grown Arowanas, will have a footprint of 8 feet by 4 feet. You'd need a very large living space to be able to accommodate a tank like this.

There are other negative aspects to consider: you'll need the time and commitment to maintain the quality and chemistry of that giant tank, including any necessary plant maintenance and ensuring that you have a filtration system that can adequately handle such an expansive volume of water.

You'll also need to spend money on feeding your Arowana — and don't forget to calculate in a multiplier of this cost factor if you have more than one. Many kinds of Arowanas require some kind of live food for a balanced diet and to alleviate boredom, so those who are squeamish about feeding live fish or crickets to a predator may want to rethink their choice of aquarium inhabitant.

Of course, like any pet, you'll also need to consider your Arowana's susceptibility to disease. Arowanas may get an illness or infection that requires you to treat it. This is additional time, energy, and expense that you'll take on if your Arowana is in less than perfect health. Young Arowanas in particular are at risk for numerous types of afflictions, including fatal ones.

You'll want to take all of these negative aspects into account when deciding whether you wish to purchase an Arowana. Without a doubt, these fish are one of the most unique and special inhabitants you can add to an aquarium — and if you're sure that you understand all the risks and requirements that come with owning one, you'll be richly rewarded for your efforts.

Chapter 13: Arowana Care

There's no doubt that Arowanas among the most fascinating and unique aquarium fish that you can have, and many people dream of owning one. But how do you know if owning an Arowana is right for you? Are they easy to care for, or is it a major commitment that could leave you with buyer's remorse?

Many fishkeepers who own Arowanas report that the fish themselves are relatively simple to care for; they tend to be easier to feed than some other types of predatory fish, such as oscars, and with some exceptions they're generally fairly hardy and not susceptible to a great deal of common diseases, as long as the tank is well-maintained. Keeping up with regular water changes and tank maintenance is necessary for keeping any type of fish, but Arowanas don't have any exceptional requirements or demands of their owners as far as water chemistry.

In general, the biggest commitment when it comes to purchasing an Arowana is money and space. Arowanas themselves can be very expensive; while prices for small juvenile silver Arowanas can be as low as $30 in some areas, the price increases rapidly for larger fish and rarer species. High-grade adult platinum silver Arowanas, for example, can sell for an astonishing $400,000.

Beyond the cost of the fish itself, you'll also need to supply a tank; because Arowanas get so big (up to 36 inches in many cases), most of them require tanks of at least 250 gallons all the way up to 600 gallons. You'll need to filter all that water, which will require a significant investment for a quality, high-efficiency filtration system. You'll also need to purchase any chemicals you need, including a dechlorinator or water conditioner, to ensure that the water is safe for your aquarium. Additional expenses include the cost to feed your Arowana a varied diet, which will include pellets, live food, and frozen food. In most cases, you'll also want to provide rocks, driftwood, and plenty of plants to simulate the Arowana's habitat and help create a natural aesthetic to your aquarium. All of that can total up very quickly — so for most people, the hardest part about caring for an Arowana will be coming up with the money to meet all of this extraordinary fish's needs.

As you can see, Arowanas are not necessarily difficult to take care of *per se*, but that doesn't mean that you should go out and buy one until you've put in some serious research and planning.

Chapter 14: Arowana Fish Tank

Not all Arowanas are created equal. Certain types of Arowana will have specific needs, whether that be for temperature, diet, water chemistry, or the tank that they live in. For Arowanas, the footprint, or dimensions, of the tank can be even more important than the gallon requirement. As surface feeders, Arowanas require plenty of lateral swimming space, so be sure to avoid tall tanks that are deep but narrow.

The tank is the most important part of keeping a happy and healthy Arowana, so take a look at this guide, broken down by Arowana species, to help you know exactly what your fish needs from you.

Platinum Arowana

Minimum tank size: 8 feet x 3 feet x 2 feet for an adult Arowana. Like all Arowanas, Platinums are generally very active swimmers, and determined jumpers — so be sure your tank has a heavy lid in place to keep your prized Platinum Arowana off of the floor. While driftwood and plants can enhance the naturalistic appearance of your aquarium, try to keep these elements towards the sides and bottom of the tank so that they don't interfere with your Platinum's swimming space. Because they are such prized centerpiece fish, Platinums are most commonly kept in the tank alone, although it may be possible to include plecos or other bottom-dwelling fish in a Platinum Arowana aquarium.

Silver Arowana

Minimum tank size: 8 feet x 3 feet x 2 feet for an adult Arowana. There have been reports of silver Arowanas in the wild that reach up to four feet in length, although in an aquarium setting they rarely exceed three feet. Because of their impressive size and high activity level, silver Arowanas are particularly at risk of injuring themselves by slamming into the tank walls. They are such strong jumpers that they regularly injure themselves by jumping into the aquarium lid, or worse yet, ending up on the floor. This makes it all the more important to have an appropriately sized tank for your silver Arowana. Silvers grow very quickly, so if you purchase a silver while it's small, be prepared to upgrade your tank as soon as possible.

Black or Blue Arowana

Minimum tank size: 8 feet x 3 feet x 2 feet for an adult Arowana. Black Arowanas have a tendency to be slightly smaller than silvers when fully grown, but they are often kept together in the same tank and sometimes even sold together. Despite their smaller physique, blue and black Arowanas will still benefit from a tank with plenty of open swimming space. Both black and blue Arowanas are generally more expensive than silvers, although both are readily available in most areas.

Australian Arowana (Jardini Arowana and Leichardti Arowana)

Minimum tank size: 6 feet x 2.5 feet x 2 feet for a fully-grown Arowana. Australian Arowanas, sometimes known as Jardini Arowanas, Leichardti Arowanas, or simply jugs, are widely available, and most are priced higher than silvers but less than black Arowanas. Australian Arowanas are known to be somewhat more aggressive than other types, so if you plan to have an Australian Arowana sharing a tank with other species, you may want to consider an even larger aquarium.

Asian Arowana

Minimum tank size: 6 feet x 2.5 feet x 2 feet for an adult Arowana. These Arowanas are illegal to own in the United States and Australia. While they can reach three feet in the wild, they typically stay a little smaller in captivity, often capping out around two and a half feet. Asian Arowanas are known to have the most variability in both coloration and aggression compared to the other species of Arowanas. Because individual temperament can vary so widely, be cautious of adding tankmates to an Asian Arowana's aquarium until you have an idea of how it will react.

Chapter 15: Tank-mates and Tank Decorations for an Arowana

Because of their huge size and notoriously aggressive temperament, fully-grown Arowanas are most commonly kept in a tank by themselves. However, that doesn't mean it's impossible to keep Arowanas with other fish if you wish to do so.

If you want to provide an Arowana with tank-mates (that aren't just the Arowana's dinner), they should be relatively calm fish who tend to occupy the bottom third of the tank. Since the Arowana will typically stay near the surface, this provides the best likelihood that the fish will stay out of each other's way. Avoid very small fish; anything that can fit in the Arowana's mouth is at risk. Aggressive or forceful fish that are prone to fin-nipping are best avoided, lest they cause damage to the Arowana's sensitive barbels. Large clown knifefish, pacu, plecostomus (commonly known as plecos), oscars, green terror cichlids, mid-sized tetras, tinfoil barbs, and other semi-aggressive fish have all been successfully housed with Arowanas.

What kinds of decorations or embellishments should you include in your Arowana's tank? Substrate is one important consideration when you're setting up your tank. For Arowanas, gravel is ideal, preferably with black or dark-colored rocks. Live aquarium plants, such as Amazon swords or giant vallisneria, will make perfect additions to an Arowana tank. Remember that Arowanas need all the space they can get at the top of the tank, so try to keep any tank decorations off to the side and plants trimmed to a reasonable length so that the top third of the tank remains unobstructed.

Chapter 16: Arowana Feeding

In the wild, Arowanas have been reported to eat just about anything that fits in their mouths, including other fish, lizards, small rodents, and even birds and bats on occasion. While wild Arowanas sometimes eat small amounts of plant matter, they are generally considered carnivores who primarily eat fish and insects.

In captivity, all types of Arowanas will generally eat a diet that combines pellets or food sticks as as a staple with an assortment of frozen and dried foods, including shrimp, krill, tubifex worms, bloodworms, nightcrawlers, and crickets. Live feeder fish, live shrimp, live crickets, and even small live frogs can be fed to an adult Arowana from time to time. None of these foods taken alone will provide an Arowana with all the nutrition it needs, so a varied diet is a must. With a little patience, you can even teach your Arowana to eat out of your hand!

Here's a handy cheat sheet to an Arowana's diet and eating habits:

- **Eating habits:** Primarily carnivore
- **Drop (sinking) food:** No, or very rarely
- **Tablets, pellets, or food sticks:** Yes, these will comprise the majority of the Arowana's diet
- **Live foods:** Yes, often
- **Frozen or dried foods:** Yes, often

- **Vegetables:** No, or rarely
- **Feeding intervals:** Juveniles can be fed up to three times a day. Adults can be fed once a day or once every other day, depending on their diet. (Arowana pellets or food sticks can be given everyday.)

Pretty simple, right? Let's expand on this basic overview a little further.

We mentioned that both live and frozen/dried foods are acceptable for Arowanas. There's a trade-off here; live foods, like shrimp, krill, etc,, tend to be more nutritious than their dried or frozen counterparts, but they also come with a substantial risk of introducing infections or disease to your Arowana's habitat. You can control for this risk by buying your Arowana's sustenance from a reputable pet store and isolating the live food for several days before you give it to your Arowana. This interim period can help you determine if there's anything off about the live food; if it still looks healthy after a few days, then you're free to give it to your Arowana. Isolating store-bought live food is especially important for feeder fish or frogs, as these carry the highest risk of disease.

There's a great range of food that you can give to your Arowana, but not all types of food are appropriate for every stage of an

Arowana's life. Here's a general guide to different types of food for juvenile Arowanas, mid-sized Arowanas, and full-grown Arowanas. (This information applies to all species of Arowanas.)

Juvenile Arowanas

- **Dried Plankton:**

Dried plankton contains high levels of karotene, which helps improve the coloration of Arowanas (particularly red Asian Arowanas). Plankton is typically a favorite of Arowanas. Remember to remove any sharp shell fragments or exoskeleton that gets mixed in with dried plankton, as these things can damage your Arowana's stomach.

- **Dried Bloodworms:**

Dried bloodworms are extremely nutritious. If you need to compel your new juvenile aro to eat, dried bloodworms are a perfect place to start; they're irresistible to most young Arowanas. Dried bloodworms usually float on the surface of the water, which make them especially easy food to give your fish.

- **Small Crickets:**

Arowanas can never resist crickets. However, they contain very little nutrition on their own; you can bulk them up by feeding carrots to the crickets before feeding the crickets to your fish. Be sure to get baby crickets, as full-size crickets will have a harder exoskeleton and may be too big for a juvenile aro to eat.

- **Hikari Food Sticks (broken into small pieces):**

Young Arowanas may resist eating food sticks or pellets at first, but it's important to get them accustomed to this type of food. It may take a few tries for aros to willingly accept non-live food. Any food sticks or pellets will typically work for this purpose, not just Hikari food sticks; just be sure the pieces are small enough that the Arowana can swallow them without a problem.

- **Frozen Shrimp (de-shelled, defrosted and cut into small pieces):**

Ensure that you completely remove the shell and defrost the shrimp before offering it to your Arowana; hard or sharp pieces of food can cause damage to young aros.

Mid-Sized Arowanas

Mid-sized Arowanas can be fed all of the foods mentioned in the previous section, in addition to the following:

- **Hikari Aro Food Sticks:**

At this size, your aro can eat full sticks without needing them broken up. By now, food sticks or pellets should be your fish's staple form of food (but again, be sure to offer a variety of other "treats" as well).

- **Cockroaches:**

Arowanas enjoy cockroaches, although they provide little nutrition. Be sure to avoid cockroaches that are already dead and always isolate a cockroach for several days before giving it to your aro in case the cockroach has been affected by any kind of pesticide, which can be extremely harmful if consumed by your fish.

- **Centipedes:**

Centipedes are extremely nutritious for an Arowana, but live centipedes are hard to find in most places. In Asia, centipedes are regularly offered to aros in order to improve coloration. Be cautious of dead centipedes in case they've been affected by pesticide.

- **Crickets:**

There's no real need for your Arowana to ever eat crickets as they provide no valuable nutrients to speak of, but aros do love them. If your Arowana is sick or is refusing to eat, crickets can be an ideal way to entice the fish to get at least some sustenance. Feed carrots to the crickets before providing them to the Arowana to improve nutrition.

- **Live Fish:**

Feeder goldfish, small koi, and infant catfish are all acceptable fish for your Arowana to eat. However, be aware that introducing any fish, especially feeder fish, into your Arowana's tank carries the risk of disease or infection. Always isolate feeder fish for several days and watch carefully for signs of disease before you add the fish to your aro's tank. If you need to administer medicine to your Arowana, you can give it to the feeder fish just before placing it in the Arowana's tank. Goldfish, although cheap and accessible, are not especially healthy for Arowanas and should be given sparingly.

- **Mealworms:**

Mealworms contain an abundance of karotene, which can improve the coloration on Arowanas and bring out vivid patterns on the fish's scales.

- **Filets:**

If you have some extra fish filet from dinner the other night, your Arowana can help you take care of the leftovers. This shouldn't be a staple, but as an occasional treat, it won't do any harm.

- **Mussels, Oysters, and Cockles:**

Many Arowanas will enjoy shellfish occasionally. Mussels, clams, oysters and cockles are all acceptable food for your Arowana, but offer them sparingly.

- **Anchovies:**

Anchovies should be very limited in your aro's diet, as they're extremely high in salt, but they have been known to clear up stomach ailments in Arowanas.

- **Bloodworms:**

Avoid live bloodworms, as they often host parasites that can make your Arowana extremely sick if ingested. Dried or frozen bloodworms should not be a staple, but Arowanas love them as a supplement to their standard diet.

- **Nightcrawlers:_____**

Thanks to their diet of rotting plant and organic material, nightcrawlers provide a rich source of minerals for your Arowana.

Full-grown Arowanas

Arowanas in this category can be fed any of the foods in the preceding categories, as well as the following:

- **Adult Shrimp or Prawns:**

A full-grown Arowana should have no trouble eating full shrimp, shell and all. However, it should be noted that a sharp shrimp tail can have serious, even fatal, consequences if it creates a wound in the Arowana's stomach. If this concerns you, you can remove the tail and/or shell before offering the shrimp to your aro.

- **Frogs:**

Very small frogs can usually be provided to mid-sized Arowanas without a problem, but to be on the safe side, we've included it on the list for fully grown Arowanas only. Be extremely careful that any frogs you feed to your Arowana are non-toxic, and always isolate feeder frogs for several days before adding them to your Arowana's tank.

Chapter 17: Costs Associated with Buying and Owning an Arowana

The cost of purchasing an Arowana will vary greatly depending on what type of Arowana you want. Particularly if you live outside of Asia, supply of these fish is likely to be limited, and in the United States, restricted species of Asian Arowana will not be available for purchase at all. Generally, if you want a healthy, full-grown Arowana, you'll pay hundreds or thousands of dollars nearly anywhere you go. This is especially true if you're interested in a relatively rare species like the blue or black Arowana. If, however, you're willing to raise a younger Arowana to full size, you'll be able to find juvenile Arowanas at a much lower price point.

Keeping an aquarium isn't necessarily an inexpensive hobby under any circumstances. For fish like Arowanas, the costs start to pile up especially quickly. A 125 gallon aquarium can easily run $500 (USD), and most Arowana species can even outgrow that. The truly gigantic tanks that are required for full-sized, three-foot-long Arowanas — which can be up to 600 gallons — often need to be custom-made. When it comes to cost, keeping Arowanas leaves very little room to cut corners.

Costs for Arowanas vary widely by region, availability, time of year, retailer markup, and more. However, to give you a general idea, here's a brief breakdown of the prices to purchase an Arowana from a typical fish store based in the U.S.:

- 2 – 3" silver $29.99 – $49.99
- 4 – 5" silver $59.99 – $79.99
- 6 – 7" silver $89.99 – $119.99
- 8 – 10" silver $129.99 – $149.99
- 2 – 3" jardini (Australian Arowana) $59.99 – $79.99
- 4 – 5" jardini (Australian Arowana) $89.99 – $99.99
- 6 – 8" jardini (Australian Arowana) $119.99 – $149.99
- 2 – 3.5" black or blue $149.99 – $199.99
- 5 – 6" black or blue $225 – $269.99
- 8 – 10" black or blue $299.99+
- 2 – 3" leichardtii $249.99 – $299.99

The tank and the fish are far from the only things you'll need to purchase. For example, the filtration system for a 300 gallon tank could easily range into the hundreds of dollars on its own. You'll also need to purchase substrate to cover the bottom of the tank, one or more heaters (which will also be very costly for an aquarium of that size), an aquarium lid, a tank thermometer, an aquarium light, and, in most cases, you'll also want live plants so your tank doesn't just look like a glass box with water in it. A single Amazon sword plant can cost $5 – $8; consider how many plants you'll need in a 300 gallon tank before it looks the way you want it to.

The moral of the story is that even if you purchase a juvenile silver Arowana — which are about the cheapest Arowanas available on the market — by the time you buy all of the other trappings you'll need to keep your fish healthy, your total is almost guaranteed to come in over a thousand dollars, and could be much more.

Chapter 18: Where to Buy Arowanas in the US and the UK

The best place to get an Arowana is your local fish store. Often abbreviated LFS in the aquarium trade, these shops are often locally-owned and can be an extremely helpful resource, not only when you're purchasing the Arowana but also in helping you set up your tank or addressing any problems that arise after you bring the fish home. In general, all metropolitan areas will have at least one LFS. Try a quick search on your favorite search engine for "local fish store near me," and you should be able to find what you need within driving distance.

If you don't have an LFS near you, or if you don't like the selection available at your LFS, online retailers are another option when it comes to purchasing an Arowana. Online retailers offer up a broad range of opportunities to buy fish that you may not otherwise be able to access. However, be sure to do your research before you decide to buy from a company; especially with Arowanas, because they can come with such a steep price tag and because of the legal restrictions surrounding certain types of Arowanas, you'll want to be absolutely sure that you're dealing with a reputable company. AquariumFish.net is a terrific place to start in your online shopping endeavors. This company is owned by two brothers who have been in the fish business for more than 40 years. They have a seasonal selection of Arowanas and hundreds of other fish for sale.

An important consideration when ordering fish online is how they will be shipped to you. For buyers in much of the U.S. and United Kingdom, cold weather can be very dangerous for fish that are being transported via postal service. Arowanas, like most aquarium fish, are native to a tropical climate, which means they need a constant tropical water temperature to survive. If the box containing your fish is delivered to your door and you're not there to pick it up, the package could easily sit outside for several hours. Low temperatures could kill your fish very quickly in this scenario. Most online retailers will only ship fish during certain seasons to prevent this from happening, but it's still worth some due diligence on your part. If you know that an unseasonable cold snap is on the way, wait to order your fish until warmer temperatures return.

Besides an LFS or an online retailer, another fantastic option for purchasing an Arowana is to connect with someone who is trying to re-home theirs. This is an all-too-common scenario; a fishkeeper purchases an Arowana while it's small, and quickly realizes just how big it's going to get. If you can find someone, either through word of mouth or through an online platform like Craigslist, who is looking to get rid of an Arowana, you have the opportunity for a mutually beneficial arrangement. You might be able to score a great deal on the fish because the seller is happy to get rid of it, and the seller can rest easy knowing the fish is going to a good home.

Chapter 19: Training Your Arowana

Many people wonder whether Arowanas can be trained in any meaningful way, particularly because these fish are so long-lived (20 years and beyond with proper care). There are aspects in which Arowanas absolutely can be trained. For example, experts state that Arowanas not only can but *should* be trained to eat at a certain time each day, which can be done easily by feeding the Arowana on a consistent schedule. This can be particularly important if your Arowana shares the tank with any smaller species, as the expectation of a regular meal will minimize the risk of the Arowana snacking on its tank-mates.

Besides training your Arowana *when* to eat, you can also train your Arowana *what* to eat. In the wild, Arowanas are hunters; they are capable of jumping up to 6 feet in the air to capture insects, frogs, or even low-flying bats and birds in some cases. Because wild Arowanas are carnivores, these fish are evolutionarily designed not to see something as food unless it's moving.

The result is that most young Arowanas are not willing to eat food sticks or pellets without being trained to accept them. Juvenile Arowanas often start out eating things like bloodworm, krill, and shrimp, either live or frozen. Even when frozen or dried, these foods mimic the shape and smell of the Arowana's natural food, and so Arowanas generally have no problem eating them.

In order to train your Arowana to accept pellets or food sticks (which will make up the bulk of the fish's diet once it reaches adulthood), most fishkeepers simply refraining from feeding the Arowana for several days, or up to a week in some cases, before offering the Arowana pellets or sticks. Some people have also had success soaking the pellets in water along with the young Arowana's preferred food, particularly krill or bloodworms, and then offering these pellets as a transition food to wean the Arowana off of its original diet. Once the Arowana has been trained to regularly accept pellets or food sticks, you can supplement its diet with other sources of nutrition, including all of the suggestions in Chapter 16: Feeding Your Arowana.

Remember that if you offer your Arowana a pellet or food stick and the Arowana refuses to eat it, you'll want to scoop it out of the tank immediately, as decaying food in the water can have an extremely adverse effect on the water chemistry.

Arowanas can be trained in other ways, too. Many fishkeepers have reported that they have, albeit inadvertently, trained their Arowanas to recognize their face. In many cases, Arowanas will react differently when they see their owner (or at least the person who regularly feeds them) compared to when they see a different person enter the room. For example, your Arowana may immediately swim up to the side of the tank when you step into the room, but it will shyly retreat into a corner if someone else comes near the tank.

Additionally, some aquarium hobbyists have been able to train their Arowanas to eat out of their hand. To do this, you'll need to wait until your Arowana is comfortable in its environment, preferably after you've had it for several weeks and it's settled into its home. Then, avoid feeding your Arowana for a few days (Arowanas can go without food for much longer than this; skipping feedings for a few days will have no adverse effect on the Arowana's health). Choose a food that your Arowana enjoys, like mealworms or crickets, and place it in your hand. Make sure the room is relatively dark, as this will help keep your Arowana calm. Then simply float your hand on the surface of the water and remain very steady to avoid spooking the fish. The Arowana should swim up and eat the food out of your hand.

It may take a few tries to entice your Arowana to work with you on this, but this can be quite a rewarding and thrilling experience — particularly as your Arowana continues to grow. Imagine a beautiful 30" fish swimming right up to eat out of your hand!

Chapter 20: Arowana Lifespan

Lifespan for Arowanas can vary, with the biggest factor being how well the fishkeeper takes care of them. Sadly, many Arowanas do not live past three to five years, simply because their owners are unprepared to take care of these unique fish. However, most aquarium hobbyists agree that if they are adequately cared for, the lifespan for Arowanas is easily around 15-20 years. Some hobbyists have reported that it's not uncommon for a healthy Arowana in a expertly-maintained aquarium to live up to 30 years.

At the very outside, there have even been some reports of Arowanas living up to 50 years old. These reports are uncorroborated, and it's difficult to track this information since the Arowana's popularity as an aquarium fish is relatively new. But the important takeaway here is that Arowanas are not a casual commitment; they are more than capable of living longer than an average cat or dog. If you take care of it well, this fish could be with you for a very long time, so think carefully before you decide to get one.

Chapter 21: Common Arowana Afflictions and How to Cure Them

Anytime an animal is pulled from its natural habitat and placed in a simulated environment, there's an increased risk of infection or disease. Particularly when fish are moved to a new tank, high levels of anxiety and stress can overburden a fish's immune system and lead to a variety of afflictions. If the owner is not vigilant in monitoring the water quality and all the other important aspects of tank maintenance, the fish can become even more stressed until sickness is the almost inevitable result.

It's best to keep your Arowana in good health in the first place whenever possible. But if an Arowana does become sick, it's important to know what steps you can take to quickly resolve the problem and provide the Arowana with everything it needs to make a full recovery. While Arowanas are typically fairly hardy and resistant to disease, there are any number of factors that can lead to your fish becoming sick. Review the list below for some of the most common afflictions that impact Arowanas, their symptoms, and their treatments.

Ascites

Cause:

Ascites (excessive fluid build-up in the abdomen) normally occurs in young Arowanas. Most commonly, it's caused by eating a sharp fragment of bone or shell that creates a wound in the Arowana's stomach. This wound can become infected with a bacteria called vibrio, which in turn causes ascites.

Symptoms:

The Arowana will display a visibly swelled stomach. After the condition has progressed to the point where water can't be removed from the body, the fish's swim bladder will be compressed by the stomach. As a result, the Arowana may display problems adjusting itself in the water; it may shake or struggle while it moves.

Treatment:

The likelihood of curing ascites is low. The best course of action is to have the Arowana to take an antibacterial sulfonamide orally. Increase the frequency of water changes and raise the temperature of the tank by a few degrees.

Tilted (Overturned) Gills

Cause:

The most common cause of tilted gills is poor water quality. An excess of nitrates can lower the amount of oxygen in the water, which affects the fish's ability to breathe through its gills. An inadequately sized tank can also cause this condition; Arowanas need to move freely in order to breathe, and if the Arowana's movements are restricted by the space of the tank, tilted gills can result. A sudden change in the aquarium's temperature, whether hotter or colder, can also cause tilted gill covers.

Symptoms:

During the first stage, the Arowana's breathing will be fast and irregular. Next, the gill covers will appear distinctly sunken and the edges may twist upwards. In the final stages of this condition, the fish will refuse food and constantly hold its head to the surface for air. This behavior implies the inner gills have likely been damaged by infection, hindering the Arowana's ability to breathe and likely leading to death.

Treatment:

When you first see that the Arowana is not breathing well, the water should be changed immediately (20% to 25% is ideal). Every 2 to 3 days thereafter, another 20% of the water in the aquarium ought to be changed until the fish's condition improves. Air bubble stones can be added to the tank to increase oxygen levels in the water.

Shady Eyes

Cause:

This condition usually occurs because of poor water quality, due to insufficient filtration or infrequent water changes.

Symptoms:

At first, one eye may seem clouded. Gradually, a distinct filmy cover will appear over the entire eye. After a while, the eyes may swell and a blue-white fungus-like substance can cover the eyes.

If the condition is not treated, the fish could suffer from visual impairment or death.

Treatment:

As soon as you see indications of shady eye, one third of the water should be changed and aquarium salt should be added. Water temperature should be increased to roughly 89° Fahrenheit. Watch the Arowana closely for two days. If the issue continues, continue to do 25% water changes every three days and continue to add aquarium salt. For advanced cases, visit an LFS for a medicated bath solution. Each of these products will have its own set of instructions; follow them closely. By the time the eyes show signs of mildew-like growth, recuperation may take three to five months. If the Arowana pulls through, the eyes may seem smaller than they were previously, but this is normal and should not cause a problem as long as the symptoms have been resolved.

Jutting Scales Disease

Cause:

Dirty water or rapid temperature fluctuations have been known to cause jutting scales disease. This affliction almost always affects juvenile Arowanas rather than full-grown adults.

Symptoms:

At first, a few scales will tilt up and away from the body. Blood may be visible at the base of the tilted scales. If the condition is not resolved at this stage, an increasing number of scales will begin to tilt. This leaves the fish extremely vulnerable to attack by microorganisms and infection. Eventually, the scales may drop off, which is almost certain to cause death.

Treatment:

Add aquarium salt and increase the water temperature to roughly 89° Fahrenheit. Change 25% of the water every three to four days. Be sure to temperature-match the new water with the tank water. If the issue persists, add copper sulfate medication to the water (be sure to follow the product instructions closely).

Decaying Gills Disease (also known as Gill Rot)

Cause:

Decaying gills are almost always the result of insufficient water changes creating poor water quality. The condition is caused by a tiny parasite that infects the Arowana's gills and prevents the fish from adequately taking in oxygen. These parasites duplicate rapidly at 77° F. This ailment is exceptionally infectious.

Symptoms:

The fish is breathing quickly and its color is dull. The fish may appear lethargic, and the gills may appear inflamed or irritated. Gray, necrotic tissue may be visible on the gills at an advanced stage.

Treatment:

See treatment for white spots disease; the process will be identical for curing gill rot.

Red Spots Disease

Cause:

This is frequently viewed as a fatal sickness and it generally affects juvenile Arowanas. It occurs when a spore penetrates the skin of a fish and causes deep ulcers, which can ultimately reach all the way to the muscle of the fish.

Symptoms:

Red spots, small at first, appear on the back half of the body. These spots gradually swell and spread, affecting the surrounding tissue. Eventually the ulcers may become so deep that they expose the muscle, bone, or viscera underneath.

Treatment:

Cold water temperatures suppress fish's immune systems; increase the temperature to 89° F and, if possible, apply a topical antiseptic iodophore solution. This will improve the chances of recovery if done early enough.

Parasites

Fish lice

Cause:

Parasites are most often transmitted to Arowanas through live feeder fish. It's very common for feeder fish to carry disease or infection, so be sure to isolate any live food for several days to check for signs of ill health before providing the food to your

Arowana.

Symptoms:

Roughly 3 to 5 mm long, this parasite can be seen with the naked eye on the outside of the fish's body. It has a needle-like structure at the mouth to suck blood from the fish, causing the fish to appear pale. The fish will show signs of discomfort, including scratching on rocks or the bottom of the aquarium while it tries to rid itself of the parasite.

Treatment:

Most parasites can be killed with copper sulfate drugs. A copper sulfate solution can be added directly to the tank water. Be extremely cautious with this treatment; copper will kill parasites, but too much will kill your fish as well.

Note: Once an Arowana has suffered from parasites, the entire tank must be thoroughly cleaned to prevent a recurrence.

Water Mycosis

Cause:

Parasites are most often transmitted to Arowanas through live feeder fish. It's very common for feeder fish to carry disease or infection, so be sure to isolate any live food for several days to check for signs of ill health before providing the food to your Arowana.

Symptoms:

A white substance with a cotton-like texture will appear over an injury on the fish's body. The Arowana will often appear aggressive and temperamental, and may be seen rubbing its budding on rocks or the substrate. Water mycosis can be fatal, as infected fish tend to lose their appetite and become increasingly susceptible to other diseases.

Treatment:

First, try including aquarium salt in the water, up to a concentration of 1%. Then apply disinfectant to the injury. Another option is the use of malachite green, but be extremely cautious as this substance is highly toxic in anything above the recommended dosage.

Anchor Worm

Cause:

Parasites are most often transmitted to Arowanas through live feeder fish. It's very common for feeder fish to carry disease or infection, so be sure to isolate any live food for several days to check for signs of ill health before providing the food to your Arowana.

Symptoms:

Anchor worm is most commonly found around the blades or fins, or inside of the fish. The head of the worm is forked and it sucks nutrients directly from the fish's body. The length of this parasite is around 1 cm. The affected area will typically show signs of redness and swelling with hints of blood. After that, tissue may turn gray and dead-looking as rot sets in. An infected fish will frequently rub its body on rocks or the substrate, and will generally have no appetite.

Treatment:

Most parasites can be killed with copper sulfate drugs. A copper sulfate solution can be added directly to the tank water. Be extremely cautious with this treatment; copper will kill parasites, but too much will kill your fish as well.

Note: Once an Arowana has suffered from parasites, the entire tank must be thoroughly cleaned to prevent a recurrence.

White Spot Disease (Ich)

Cause:

This ailment is extremely common among many types of fish. Ich is a parasite that will attack fish with poor immune systems and low resistance. Infected fish will show small white dots like grains of sand on their body, particularly near the gills.

Symptoms:

At introductory stage, the infection influences principally the balances. The fish that has been tainted with this infection tends to scratch itself against the sides or base of the aquarium to free its tingle. Its craving falls apart enormously and balance closes begins to decay. In conclusion when it assaults the gills, the fish may bite the dust.

Treatment: Increase the temperature up to 86° Fahrenheit, or 89° if your Arowana can handle it. Perform 25% water changes daily, and use aquarium salt until the situation improves.

Chapter 22: Arowana Breeding

Arowanas are typically only bred in large commercial facilities that have dedicated space for extremely large tanks, or even whole lakes, in which fry can grow out. Even though it is not generally done by ordinary aquarists, breeding Arowanas is a fascinating process.

Arowana are mouthbrooders, with the males typically holding the eggs or fry for no less than two months. The eggs are huge relative to comparable species, at 4 to 5 mm in size. Broods can vary widely in number, ranging anywhere from 12 to 80 fry. When breeding Arowanas, the fry are typically separated from the parents as soon as possible. This can be achieved by prying open the mouth of the paternal fish and gathering the fry, or simply by waiting until they are discharged normally. Arowana breeders typically do this for two reasons: it reduces the likelihood of the parent Arowana eating any of their young, and it speeds up the process of preparing the adult Arowana for the next breeding cycle.

The grow-out tanks for Arowana fry are typically very large. Experts in the field generally recommend at least an 8-foot tank for 12 fry as a minimum. For the best possible development of the fry, it's important that they have an uncrowded space in which the Arowana fry are the largest fish present. The fry do not need to be separated immediately, although they may quickly develop a pecking order that leads to some or one of the brood taking the brunt of the aggression of its siblings.

When Arowana are born, they have a yolk sac attached to them that helps the fry through the initial stages of growth and development. Over time, the yolk sac will be reabsorbed and vanish. Breeders often send young Arowanas to pet stores with the yolk sacs still attached, although it's typically recommended that customers avoid buying Arowanas this young.

While commercial breeding of Arowanas has become a booming business, there's still a great deal of mystery surrounding Arowana breeding behavior in the wild.

Chapter 23: Forums and Online Retailers for Purchasing Supplies for Your Arowana

The information in this guide has covered every aspect of Arowana care, from tank setup to purchasing costs to recommended treatments in case your Arowana falls sick. If you're still interested in purchasing an Arowana of your own, take a look at these additional resources to help you take the next steps.

Forums:

Forums provide a wonderful community of aquarists with wide-ranging interests and experiences. If you run into any questions at any point in the process of preparing for or caring for an Arowana, there's always a friendly expert who can help you on one of these sites:

www.MonsterFishKeepers.com

www.BCAquaria.com

www.AroFanatics.com

Shopping resources:

Ready to start buying? Here are some of the best-rated online retailers for Arowanas and aquarium supplies:

www.Arowana.co.uk (United Kingdom)

www.AquariumFish.net (United States)

www.ArowanaShop.net (Canada)

You can even try your luck on www.eBay.com — many sellers are offering auctions on Arowana fish, as well as any other aquarium-related supply you could need.

Conclusion

Arowanas are some of the most remarkable aquarium fish in the world. From their beautiful form and coloration to their deadly precision in striking down prey, from the ancient legends and lore that surround the species to the devoted fascination of modern-day aquarists who are willing to pay hundreds of thousands of dollars to own just one, the Arowana is truly a one-of-a-kind creature.

This guide has covered all of the key aspects of Arowanas, including the fish's native habitat, the various types of Arowanas, the requirements for keeping one of these fish, the possible afflictions that an Arowana may develop, and much more. Whether you're a longtime aquarium hobbyist brushing up on your Arowana knowledge, or you're a beginner to the fascinating and intricate world of freshwater aquariums, we hope this guide has provided useful information for you.

The Chinese believe that the Arowana will bring peace, prosperity, and good fortune into any home they inhabit. We wish you all of that and more in your fishkeeping endeavors!

Printed in Great Britain
by Amazon

38502686R00061